INTO T GREAT WIDE OPEN

Lynn Dryden

Dedication

I would like to dedicate this book to my brave husband and soulmate Jim, "I love you millions", and to every other man in the world today who is fighting Prostate Cancer. Not forgetting all the fantastic oncologists, doctors and nursing staff who help us all, "To keep on keeping on." Also to our daughter, her family, and all of our family and friends who are a great support to us both every day.

All profits from the sale of this book will be donated to **Prostate Cancer UK** for research. For more information see https://prostatecanceruk.org.

Prostate Cancer UK is a registered charity in England and Wales (1005541) and in Scotland (SC039332). Registered company 02653887.

Published by Brilliant Publications
Unit 10
Sparrow Hall Farm
Edlesborough
Dunstable
Bedfordshire
LU6 2ES, UK

www.brilliantpublications.co.uk

The name Brilliant Publications and the logo are registered trademarks.

Written by Lynn Dryden

© Text, maps and photographs Lynn Dryden 2018
© Design Brilliant Publications 2018

Print ISBN 978-1-78317-347-1

First printed and published in the UK in 2018

CONTENTS

INTRODUCTION

I feel I must write an introduction to this book because my original intention was simply to share our experience of buying an 8-seater people carrier and either converting it into a camper van ourselves or finding someone to convert it to suit our own purposes. I then thought people might like to read about the trips we have done in the van. My purpose was to encourage anyone who has ever wanted to own a camper van, but thought it was way out of their reach, to realise their dream or at least to give them something to consider and think about.

I hope I have managed to do that; but just after I started writing this book, my husband became ill and needed treatment. As he started treatment I was ready to start writing about the road trip around Scotland that we had done in Ruby, our camper van. Talking about our road trip focussed our minds elsewhere and we had great fun talking about each place we had visited. It was weird because we each had a different memory for the same place.

At that point in time any stay-away trips were out of the question but we contented ourselves with days away exploring our own beautiful Northumberland coast. Our days away in winter and spring being so close to nature lifted our spirits and this, coupled with reliving our previous trips when writing this book, helped us to get our lives back and gave us the strength and determination to get back on the road. Anne Frank who is admired by millions of people all over the world said, "I firmly believe that nature brings solace in all troubles." She had a wonderful young mind, heart and soul to say something so profound and so true.

Although my husband will always need treatment for his cancer, writing this book has helped him and I through a very worrying time and, even though we have setbacks, we are trying to get back on the road and we hope to enjoy many more adventures.

All profits from the sale of this book will be donated to **Prostate Cancer UK** for research.

Lynn Dryden

Chapter 1
INTO THE GREAT WIDE OPEN WITH RUBY
The dream that came from Tokyo to Tranent

I'd seen all the adverts for camper vans and I knew what a fun way they were to travel. We had hired them when Tessa (our daughter) was small and we had enjoyed some great holidays. In fact, as we got older, we hired one almost every year and had a brilliant time. It was an extra treat added to all our other holidays. We had done fantastic road trips in the US along Highway 101 in Oregon and Washington State and in the southern states of Georgia and Tennessee, taking in places like Atlanta, Chattanooga, Nashville and Memphis as we both love music. But the freedom and peace that "getting out into the great wide open", as Tom Petty said, really touched our hearts. It was time "to put up or shut up" as it were, because we were at a crossroads; we had both retired and yearned for the freedom that only a camper van could give us.

We had thought about buying a van of our own but, thinking sensibly, a big van was out of our league unless we won the lottery and, to be honest, there were places we had visited and wanted to return to where a big van had been a liability, in spite of the luxury they gave you. Also I would have hated to buy a van that was too big for our drive as it would have to go into storage which would cost more money. It also meant that the freedom of just being able to make a decision to up and go away when we wanted would be minimised. So – hand on heart – I can say that I wanted a van that I would feel comfortable driving on single track roads, that I could keep on our drive and one that I could park and enjoy driving whenever I wanted. Every time I got into it, I wanted to feel excited about the journey as well as the destination.

Then I read about the Mazda Bongo craze online. Lots of people had been buying Bongo vans, which were currently being imported from Japan. Some people told good stories and other people talked about how they had bought what Geordies would call, "a good looking nowt." I had never seen a Bongo, but I found lots online and the idea of being able to turn one into a camper van to suit our taste appealed to me. I was also very aware of having to ensure whatever we were going to buy would have to be checked over very carefully. I had also seen Fiat Doblos and Renault Kangoos and Trafics transformed into camper vans and people who had made a really good job of their conversions.

At this point, it is important to tell you that I had had similar ideas myself, along with the idea of asking Jim to buy me a tear drop caravan that my mini could pull, as well as various types of other towable pods I had seen online. I didn't want a caravan because it would take up too much space on the drive and, to be honest, I never saw us two in a caravan. Poor Jim, I was always wittering on about how fantastic having a Bongo or any van would be, so – after weeks of wittering (and for a bit of peace) – he agreed to take me to see some Bongos at a dealer nearby.

Although the idea got my imagination going, I was neither impatient nor desperate to buy the first one we saw. In fact, when I saw the layout of some vans, I knew I hadn't found what I was after. Some had extending roofs which were shabby and would need replacing, there was evidence of rain leaking in; some smelled damp, while others reeked of smoke. Also, the prices were crazy for the amount of work needed – most were almost £10,000. These were old vans and some had high mileages and, while a conversion was offered for a crazy price, it was everything I personally didn't want. I was a bit gutted to say the least. I was very disappointed to realise we had a nigh on impossible job on our hands. It was so tempting to give up the idea and I almost gave up then, but I had a feeling that I would know when the right van came along and I wasn't bothered about how long it might take to find it. I looked at hundreds online, but none of them seemed right; most of them sounded too good to be true. Then I found an advert for vans in Scotland, near a place where our family holidayed when we were young. I thought this might be a good omen as this was weeks after our first visit to look at vans. The garage had a good reputation so off we went. Needless to say there were three Bongos, a Toyota Regius (which was already converted) and a VW that was only about 4 years old and pristine. The VW was very nice, but way out of our league. On closer inspection, I preferred the Toyota to the Bongo, simply for the layout as it suited us better. However, the conversion wasn't to our taste. We came away disappointed. I was amazed at my own restraint and inability to rush into buying – had I grown up and gained patience in my old age? Alistair (the salesman) asked us what we were looking for, so I told him , "I wanted a van with a low mileage, good engine, good bodywork and a clean interior that didn't smell of smoke." This caused him much hilarity and he said I was asking a bit too much and laughed but he also said, "Well in this business you never know."

We returned home and the search for the Holy Grail was put on hold temporarily but, three days later, Alistair rang me. Unbeknownst to him we had nicknamed him Ali Bongo because he sold Bongos as well as cars and caravans. He said he was expecting a van in that day that looked perfect on paper. He said all the usual stuff, like he had "never had one like this" and it was "too good an opportunity to miss" – all the usual blurb – but the cynic in me said, "Thanks for ringing, but I am busy, but to let me know the next time." Then Jim looked at me, amazed at how I hadn't questioned him about the van. Maybe I was being too cynical? So I rang back and an 100 mile drive later, we were back in Tranent by 5 pm that afternoon.

Did I say I wasn't impatient and that I was very happy for us to wait for what we wanted? Me impulsive? Never! I saw the van from the outside and the inside and the underneath and it was pristine. The mechanic, John, went over it and said he had "never seen one so good." I had known as soon as I stepped into the van it was clean inside: the 8 seats were immaculate, it didn't smell of smoke or damp and the body work was clean and shiny. It was 15 years old with 40,000 miles on the clock but it was recorded as 64,000 kilometres. This van had been somebody's baby. I told Jim there and then I was ready to sell my precious Mini so it could be ours. Jim agreed with me; the van was exactly what we had been looking for. It was £5995. At that point in time, my Mini and I were joined at the hip, but the freedom the van would give us and the travel opportunities would be amazing, so I was quite happy to sell my Mini to buy the van.

Chapter 2
THE VAN
From Tranent to Tyneside

Once I had decided to sell my Mini, I agreed with Alistair that I would return in two weeks to pick up the van as it needed an MOT and it also had to be registered with the DVLA. Because the underneath of the van was so clean, he recommended having it wax oiled to protect it. This all gave me time to sell my Mini, which I did two days before I was due to pick up the van. I was so excited. It was like waiting for that special present for your birthday or Christmas.

Finally the day dawned for the pickup and I realised in a panic that I had never driven the van. Jim had driven on our first visit. What would happen if I didn't like the way it drove? What if I couldn't drive an automatic? All these troubles were running through my head. I couldn't believe I had actually bought a van I had never driven. I felt like a hen in *Chicken Run*, "I mustn't panic!"

When we got there, Jim and Ali insisted that I start off the way I meant to go on and drive it myself. I knew it was automatic and had never driven one before, so I was scared, but – hey, I had to do it – this was my baby now. So I did. Yes, I did use the wrong foot and, yes, we nearly went through the windscreen, but luckily the man behind us must have been guided by intuition and gave me a wide berth, missing the back of my new van. Thankfully Ali (though looking a bit shaken), made no comment and I was too hyper to be embarrassed.

We signed all the papers, shook hands and Ali assured us he was at the end of the phone if we ever needed help or advice. I felt like I had the best present ever. I drove 104 miles home, with Jim encouraging me and giving me the confidence I needed. We stopped for petrol in Dunbar and, after asking lots of strangers how to open the petrol cap with no luck, I had to ring Ali to ask him how. The catch was under my seat and I discovered what a big tank I had; £60 filled it but I didn't mind at all. It needed a big tank to travel on long trips.

When we got home I went straight to show my daughter and Steven, my favourite son in law, who is an excellent mechanic and who reinforced everything Alistair and John had said. My granddaughters loved all the seats and sat in every one. I then went to pick up all my family who were waiting to see my new purchase and took them for a ride – it's a family tradition. I drove to show the van to my Mam, who always blesses our cars with holy water from Lourdes – another family tradition my Nanny had started. After I had done the rounds, we went home and I made sure Jim parked his car behind my van just in case it caught somebody's eye.

The van's interior was 50 shades of grey with two seats in the front and six seats in the back, which apparently folded into a double bed. There were no curtains or blinds so my clever sister in law, Gillian, said she would make some curtains with my choice of materials. At this point in time, we needed time to get used to driving around before thinking of a trip, but we also noticed that the curtain rails which were part of the window trim had been factory fitted and discovered we needed gliders first, then hooks. The gliders were a problem. We could not get the correct size anywhere so Jim customised the ones we had bought by cutting up an old store points card, and sticking the pieces on to the gliders with super glue. It worked, so I rang Gill and told her the van was ready for curtains. She had some lovely red, white and grey checked material which she had saved specially, knowing I would like it. The curtain hanging was a special ceremony and another step closer to our first road trip. Things were taking shape!

We decided that we would sleep in the van that Friday night on our drive. We folded the seats down and put a duvet over them, then had another duvet to cover ourselves with. It was then that we discovered that the bed was a bit like a roller coaster to lie on, but we slept and crept back in the house before the neighbours were up. It had worked, but it wasn't perfect at all and we definitely needed to think about making things more comfortable. However, it didn't prevent us from looking at our big map of the British Isles and thinking about where we would like to visit. At that point in time, we actually thought we were almost ready to roll; but while our minds told us it was great, our bodies told us a different story altogether.

We had decided our maiden voyage would be a short trip to a nice site called The Barn at Beal near Lindisfarne. This trip coincided with the arrival of the Perseid Meteor Shower and also gave us the opportunity to try out a new air bed, which I thought would relieve the roller coaster feel. However we forgot that to inflate the bed we had to use a machine that made a loud screeching noise. I looked at my watch. It was 11 pm. We were helpless with laughter and really thankful we didn't have neighbours that night. Looking back, it was good we had had a good laugh because, I think I saw every Perseid meteor that flew through the sky that night. Every time Jim turned over on that air bed, I shot up in the air and was a lot closer to the stars than I wanted to be! As soon as we got home, that air bed was put away in the darkest depths of the loft, never to be used again in our van. For bedtime comfort we had no option but to go back to the drawing board. We had to face the inevitable. We were not ready yet for a long trip; we really had to make the van comfortable first.

We had bought a hook up which allowed us to use three 3-pin plugs and we had a small blow heater that Steven had given us, an electric hot plate and two Ikea clip-on lights. That was the only camping gear we had. However, the quest to obtain a comfy bed to sleep on, was soon sorted when I saw an advert for Duvalay mattress toppers specifically for camper vans. I bought two 5 cm thick memory foam toppers which fitted the van width perfectly; we also bought a double sleeping bag, a warm one.

We couldn't wait to test out our new mattress toppers so we decided to go to a Rock and Roll weekend at Skegness. We usually stay in an apartment with a group of friends but this time we were booked on the site where the event was taking place. We and our friends all dress up in the gear so we had taken our outfits for two nights of dancing. This meant we had more baggage than usual, so space was tight and this, we realised, was something we needed to sort out. It became more obvious the next morning when I noticed my bright red rock and roll petticoat was blocking our windscreen, causing much amusement to people walking past.

We had slept well, but another problem was becoming apparent. Our original mission of achieving a comfortable bed had been a success – the toppers were great – but it also highlighted the fact that we really needed space and cupboards. We couldn't really rely on the front seats as they were not hidden from public view. Our red Virgin Airline curtain separated the two front seats from the rest of the van and gave us some privacy, but anything on the front seat was visible from the outside. The huge pile of clothes and other extras we had no room for was added to throughout that weekend. We also had to get up out of bed to use the on-site toilets in the middle of the night. We needed to rethink and realised that we were on a steep learning curve. These problems, if left unsolved, would jeopardise any future trips.

We needed cupboard space but we knew if we couldn't do it ourselves, we would have to pay and we had no idea of cost. When we thought about cupboard space we realised that the seats would have to go which in turn would mean the floor would need changing. In other words – to have a fully functioning camper van, we needed to get a conversion that suited our needs but, more importantly – suited our finances. This was when I started to worry about how this would happen. How would we find someone? How would we know we were paying a fair price? How would we know they would do a good job? Could we do it? This I very much doubted. While doing a conversion adds value, it is very important to bear in mind the age of the van. You don't want a conversion that is worth more than your van. Turning the van into a camper van was a learning curve for us but we had patience and nobody could say we were not enthusiastic. I believe Ralph Waldo Emerson when he said, "Nothing great was ever achieved without enthusiasm." At that point, I knew we had quite a project to sort but I knew that one way or another, because it was something both of us really wanted – we would make it work for us.

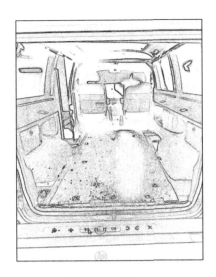

Chapter 3
MISSION IMPOSSIBLE AND REALISING THE DREAM

We knew how we wanted the inside of our van to look, but we had absolutely no idea where to look for a van conversion, so it was back to the iPad. I found a few places quite close to home and a few places too far away but that didn't mean I couldn't ring them, which I did. We also approached the company we had hired the big camper vans from over the years, who were extremely helpful in helping us to decide what we wanted and suggested other things we might need. One of the men had a pristine original VW in bright yellow and white, beautifully restored, and his colleague had a converted Bongo – both very impressive conversions done by themselves. Originally that had been our idea, but we realised anything we did would have to be agreed and passed by the DVLA; it would also determine the classification of the van.

The whole area was a bit vague, so I rang and spoke to the DVLA who were really helpful. I also spoke with my insurance company and we decided that for us, we needed to find someone to do what we wanted.

Whatever we would decide to do had to be legal, as weight and safety had to be taken into consideration. If I wanted to remove six seats but still be able to transport four people, we would need a crash tested folding seat which would seat two, allowing you to transport four people in total. The folding seat could turn into a bed to sleep two people. If we did this, it would mean our two granddaughters could share in the excitement of days out in the van. Actually finding a company who would do this was very difficult as there only seemed to be a set conversion for certain types of van, with either little or no opportunity to be either creative or basic (which some conversion people called bespoke). And, if there was, the cost was mega bucks. The prices we would have paid were almost more than what we had paid for the van or at least very near. We were rookies and people tried very hard to convince us that we really needed this special wardrobe or cupboard. I know we were new at this game, but we had a tight grip on reality and we had found nothing we liked or could really afford. This was our biggest problem yet, so we made enquiries further afield, but the conversions weren't really customised, because you had to have the full /part conversion they offered. It seemed to us that there weren't many people doing conversions who were happy to discuss our ideas, maybe because they were so basic – we just wanted a simple but neat conversion.

We were at a loss and wondering what to do next when a friend told us his friend Steve was setting himself up in business to convert camper vans, just a 40 minute drive away from us. He gave us his number. How lucky was that! We rang Steve, who actually was waiting to get premises to work in. He told us he would be happy to convert our van for us but that it might take him a few months to get started. We said there and then that we were happy to wait and he told us to think about what we wanted him to do.

He rang us when he was set up in his premises and we went along with the van. I explained about keeping the cost down and told him we would like cupboards along the side of the van, behind the driver and storage in the boot. Steve suggested a RIB crash-tested seat which folded out, then flipped comfy side up into a double bed. He asked me what colour floor we wanted and I chose the colour that was to change the van's name to Ruby. There were three or four reds to choose and I chose the brightest. Anyway, I digress! The day we dropped the van off to be converted, I was like a cat on hot bricks wondering if I would like what we had told Steve to do. It takes me months just to decide on a new paint colour for the lounge and here I was choosing how our van would look. I was very excited though, and we even had our photo taken in Steve's living room, sitting on the RIB seat which he had ordered in from somewhere in France. The conversion would take four to five weeks and we could go to look at it regularly or wait till it was finished. We decided on the latter but Steve sent us photos via WhatsApp of each stage of the conversion. He does this for all of his vans and he has photos for every conversion he has done because these are the photos you need to send to the DVLA on completion. One day the phone call came. Ruby was ready to be picked up – the day when we would become proud owners of a camper van called Ruby was here. I was so excited. Jim just laughed at me as we drove to pick up the van.

When we met Steve and his brother Mike at their workshop they were just as excited as we were, because Ruby was the first van to come out of their workshop at Northshore Custom Conversions.

When I saw the conversion I actually cried because I couldn't believe it was ours. Then when they showed us all the little gadgets on cupboards, the extra storage areas they had made and all the storage in the back of the van I cried more; we both were thrilled and amazed. Steve and Mike had gone above and beyond our expectations. Everything that turned the van into Ruby was beautifully crafted: the floor, cupboards and table top rear storage. One cupboard (which everyone thinks is a fridge!) houses our luxury item, our Porta Flush 10 toilet, nicknamed 'The Honey Bucket', for any night time visits. (Anyone who camps without one knows what it's like to walk across a field in the dark, wondering what you are putting your Crocs into. Actually, Crocs are the worst type of shoe for walking in grass in the dark; no need to explain why! Also the moths that fly around the loos on a campsite, on a night can be ginormous, so that's why we like our mini loo.)

Steve and Mike had done more than we expected at a cost which had suited us and was affordable, but the most important thing of all was they had played a massive role in helping us to achieve our lifelong dream. For us, this was going to be our second home and it was going to be on the road whenever we had the opportunity. Ruby was going to be our happy place. Picking Ruby up that day I felt like I had when other lovely events in my life had happened: like getting a brother and sister when I was young; like getting married; like having my babies; like becoming a grandma. It was a feeling of happiness you never forget and makes you smile when you think about it.

A big thank you to Steve and Mike for being so "Awesome" as my American nieces and nephews say. I also know if I want anything new in the van I can always ring them, as long as I give plenty of notice because they are so busy now and are doing great things.

Chapter 4
KITTING OUT RUBY

Now that Ruby was ready for the open road, we needed to look on the iPad for the types of things we needed for a successful trip. We also spoke to friends who either camped or had caravans. We listened and, I admit, poor Jim's ears must have been aching with all of my ideas.

It was with great excitement we went to the branch of Great Outdoors. For me it was bliss looking at all of the essentials we needed for our trip. I had only ever enjoyed shopping for clothes before this and here I was getting excited deciding on which toilet liquid to buy – did we want floral or pine? Then, as back up to our single electric cooking ring, we bought a single ring gas cooking stove. Everything we bought had to be as small as possible so we could make best use of our space. Next it was a set of chairs and a small table which we call the Hobbit set, because they are small and fold away (not because we both have hairy feet). A kettle was next, then pans, a washing-up dish, Melamine crockery and plastic storage boxes. We also bought a fleecy rug just in case the sleeping bag wasn't warm enough and a plug-in cooler bag. We already had the two Duvalay mattress toppers because the RIB bed isn't soft enough for older bones and we bought a lighter weight sleeping bag for use in the summer months.

The electric hook up we had already bought allowed us to use three devices at once. Jim devised a sponge tube that blocked the window where the hook up came in to the van. This meant on a rainy night the water didn't blow into the van.

Once I thought we had covered all our living needs, I started to think about our leisure activities. My Mam bought me a transistor radio not unlike one I had when I was 10 years old, so we wouldn't drain the battery. We also bought cheap DVDs in Tesco, Asda and charity shops to watch on Jim's computer when we were parked up. I decided to buy a few sets of battery operated lights for inside the van to give it a cosy warm glow on an evening. The two clip on lights I'd already bought from IKEA were great for reading in bed. My sister in law had brought me a working lamp from America; it was metallic red and magnetic and showed brilliant light if we needed to see something clearly. It just stuck on the wall of the van, but could be moved anywhere where it was needed.

We now had almost everything we needed for the trip, except for our music. We both have a wide taste in music. I have always loved country music and when I'm travelling I find there are loads of country songs that at times capture where you are in your life. Jim also has a love for country. I think it was our Atlanta/Chattanooga/Nashville/Memphis road trip in Georgia and Tennessee that did it. But we also both love rock, rock and roll, pop – anything really – but only I am likely to listen to rap. There is nothing so good as driving through beautiful uncrowded places, listening to music you love while being at one with nature. You will create your own play list, but here are some of the tracks we listen to when we are on our road trips:

1. Into the Great Wide Open – Tom Petty and the Heartbreakers
2. Wide Open Spaces – The Dixie Chicks
3. That's My Kind of Night – Luke Bryan
4. Born to Run – Bruce Springsteen
5. Lay Low – Josh Turner
6. I Drove All Night – Roy Orbison
7. Here I Go Again – Whitesnake
8. C'mon Everybody – Eddy Cochran
9. Radar Love – Golden Earring
10. Where the Blacktop Ends – Keith Urban
11. Missing – William Michael Morgan
12. Sweet Child o' Mine – Guns N' Roses
13. Wagon Wheel Rock – Old Crow Medicine Show
14. But for the Grace of God – Keith Urban
15. I Hope You Dance – Lee Ann Womack
16. This Is Country Music – Brad Paisley
17. 18 Till I Die – Bryan Adams
18. Route 66 – The Rolling Stones
19. Take it Easy – Eagles
20. Life Is a Highway – Rascall Flatts
21. Twice the Speed of Light – Sugarland
22. When God Fearin' Women Get the Blues – Martina McBride
23. Road Less Travelled – Lauren Alaina
24. Safe in the Arms of Love – Martina McBride
25. Born to Be Wild – Steppenwolf
26. I Take My Chances – Mary Chapin Carpenter
27. Follow Your Arrow – Kacey Musgraves
28. Good Day to Get Gone – Jason Blain
29. Livin' on a Prayer – Bon Jovi
30. It's My Life – Bon Jovi

Depending on the age of your van, it is very important to note the technology, or the lack of it, in an older van. I had a new Radio/CD player fitted which connects with your phone – you can answer the phone by pressing a button, but my iPhone doesn't connect. I have no idea why, so I have a speaker clipped onto my sun visor which does connect to my phone and when my phone rings I simply press a button and I can hear people clearly. This does not distract me in any way from my driving. However, if I wish to phone other people, I have to park up.

I have also had an alarm and immobiliser fitted which didn't break the bank. This gives me peace of mind because, after all your hard work, you don't want your van to disappear. I know these are not foolproof by any manner of means, but it's better than putting out a welcome mat. I recently bought a steering wheel lock recommended by insurance companies and the police. It's not a fail-safe device but at least it makes life a bit more difficult for someone trying to steal your van. You can buy trackers for about £300 but apparently, if thieves find them, they can throw them out of the van. You can also pay companies to track your vehicle, but this gets quite costly. I prefer to do what I can afford security wise to prevent the van being stolen and make sure I have a good up to date insurance policy. I think that's the best you can do in reality and hope you never end up in that awful situation. I would be so gutted.

I bet you are thinking, "she hasn't mentioned this or that," but I promise you, if you forget something very important on a trip, you will learn from the mistake and appreciate that item even more when you do get it.

One other thing to do is to make sure that, if you have curtains, they are lined with a blackout lining. After travelling for nearly a year, I realised one dark night while I was outside the van I could see through the Virgin Airline curtain that Jim was taking his shirt off – the shadow actually looked like a puppet show. So now our curtains are lined with blackout and there are no more accidental shadow shows.

Chapter 5
THE ROAD TRIP

Marie Forleo an American life coach once said, "The key to success is to start before you're ready." I know we did and on our first mini trip we both learnt little things we hadn't thought about, things which would make any future trips much easier. Similarly, Meister Eckhart (a German theologian, philosopher and mystic) said, "And suddenly you just know: it's time to start something new and trust the magic of beginnings." We were so trusting in those new beginnings when we set off on our very first trip with everything in place. It was a short one which we had arranged a few months earlier. We were booked at the The Barn at Beal Campsite near Lindisfarne because the next morning, on Good Friday, we were meeting up with the Lanark pilgrims, who walk from Lanark to Lindisfarne during Holy Week every year. Jim is a keen walker and wanted to complete the final step of St Cuthbert's Way, which is walking across the original causeway to the island. This can be a bit dangerous if you are not familiar with the sands. Obviously the pilgrims are and they were very happy to let us join them. We had enjoyed our night in the van and cooked porridge for breakfast which we ate sitting on our Hobbit chairs. It was a beautiful day. Once we reached the causeway, Jim decided to do the walk in true pilgrim style, barefoot whilst I, being wary of everything, erred on the side of caution and wore my new short black and white stripy wellies. The chatter all the way across was good and the people were very friendly. Both Jim and I each took our turn helping to carry the heavy wooden cross which they take with them. These people give up a week of their time every year to do this and sleep in church halls, B&Bs – anywhere they can – on their pilgrimage to Lindisfarne. Then they meet up with other pilgrims who have walked there and have a lunch and a service at the church, on Good Friday on the island. We were both happy and humbled to have mixed with such caring and wonderful people. Because we had left Ruby parked at The Barn at Beal we were unable to have lunch or attend the service because we had to catch the last bus before the tide came in. It was an experience we had both enjoyed and we were both pleased we had been given the opportunity to do this by the kind pilgrims. We would both like to do it again in the future. We knew we were ready for a longer trip now and we couldn't wait to get out on the road.

Getting ready

We are grandparents and we look after our two granddaughters Rosie and Zoé which, I have to say, we love doing. They are a real blessing, so we had to make our arrangements accordingly because these days young parents have no option but to work. However, we are very fortunate our daughter works part time and has always told us to do whatever we want and she will do her best to work around us. So we do the best we can to make everyone's life happy including ours. We had an idea we would be away about 14 days but we could have longer because we knew they would be away on holiday for 10 days. So everything was ready. We had packed the van and all that needed to go in were our clothes and two big water bottles from Asda, which we use, then top up with fresh water every day.

We use big IKEA bags for our clothes because they can be squashed underneath the back seats. Jim packs light and somehow always looks neat and has plenty to wear. I always take far too many clothes for every possible eventuality. I soon found out my bag wouldn't even fit under the seat so we had to put it on top. Looking back, I was crazy – who needs five pairs of jeans or even three fleeces, not to mention two jackets! Imelda Marcos herself would have gasped had she seen my five or six pairs of shoes. When we parked up we realised my bag was in the way of everything wherever we put it. To cut a long story short I bought a two man tent to put my clothes in and any other excessive packing ideas I'd had. I actually had to pay to pitch it on some sites as well, which was a good lesson for an excessive packer and I learnt a valuable lesson about packing which I really appreciate now. So only take what you think you need! In the words of Antoine de Saint Exupery, "He who would travel happily must travel light." That man was 100% right; maybe he did what I did and learned his lesson the hard way, or maybe he was talking about a spiritual journey – either way it makes real sense. I am so proud of the packer I have become; all I need I can put in a small soft zipped bag under the seat and still look smart.

Day 1: Wideopen to North Berwick – 97 miles

It was a momentous occasion driving out of the street thinking this was our first real adventure in our Ruby and mentally checking that we had everything we needed, albeit with a little bit of unease. But once we were out on the A1, any doubts we had about going vanished and the excitement of the open road took over. We had chosen one of our special places to stay first because it would be the starting point of our first ever trip in our own van. From being small I had always gone to North Berwick for family holidays; we all loved it. We used to stay in the Nether Abbey Hotel every year and we would play on the golden beaches or play golf with our parents who were very good golfers. We would be scared every year by the story of the North Berwick witches and Dad used to tell us about the

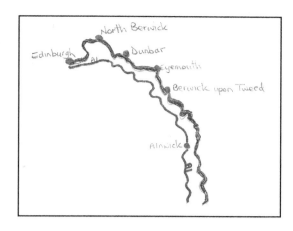

Island of Fidra influencing Robert Louis Stevenson to write *Treasure Island*. Dad must have read the book but it was also one of his favourite films; he thought Robert Newton was as excellent actor. Mam and Dad used to say it was the best place to retire to and we always used to say if the Football Pools came up that's where we would live (there wasn't the lottery back then). In the 1960s and 70s there was an open air swimming pool in the harbour which was great because it was well sheltered. We would climb the Law and stand on the top looking all around the area and out to sea. For me it was the closest place to heaven. Apparently the whale bones on the top of the Law have been replaced three times since they were first placed there in 1709 and I've since been told it is now a fibreglass replica.

Now we were driving our own van onto pitch number 84 at the Tantallon Caravan and Camping Park on what had been a beautiful day and all my happy memories were filling my head. Our pitch had good views towards Bass Rock and the air around the rock was filled with gannets. We got everything set up then walked over the golf course and along the cliffs down into town. We decided to eat out for tea then have a walk along the beautiful beaches. We tend to look for pieces of sea glass because one of my friends is an artist and uses the glass in her work and also, more recently, Jim has been making his own design of tea light holders for our garden. When we got back to Ruby, the site was bathed in pink and red light as the sun was starting to go down. We knew we would sit out and watch all the colours changing till it grew dark in this special place we had chosen to kick-start our first big trip. The night was warm, the sky was clear and there was a bright moon. When we lay in bed looking at the moon and the stars twinkling through our moon window we both realised how fortunate we were and how much we were so looking forward to the next weeks ahead.

Day 2: North Berwick to Newburn, by Upper Largo – 70 miles

We drove over the Forth Road Bridge and through rolling countryside. We stopped on the sea front at a place called Kinghorn and ate our sandwiches looking out to sea. Then we went into a café and gift shop called the Carousel, where we had a well-deserved cuppa and some cake. To get to the Forth House Caravan Site we had to drive through Lower Largo. It was a wide open rural site, so thankfully not much chance of midges. The site owners were very friendly and most of the pitches have names you would find on a golf course. All the pitches face the coast

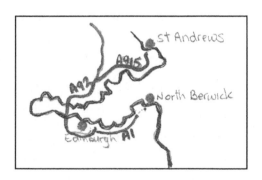

and the views were fantastic. It was very peaceful and there was a walk down a private road which I believe went into the town. Unfortunately it was quite a steep downhill walk and I didn't fancy the uphill walk back so we only walked half way. The toilets and showers are in shipping containers on site and they are unbelievable – so modern and very clean – everything you could wish for. We stayed one night, then set off the next day to St Andrews.

Day 3: Newburn, by Upper Largo to St Andrews — 12 miles

We soon arrived at Mount Melville, Craigtoun Meadows Holiday Park – which was very big and quite busy. I had never visited St Andrews but I knew I wouldn't be disappointed. From our site we could get a taxi into town almost for the price of a bus fare. This was due to an arrangement between the site and the local taxi services which was brilliant and a system that worked really well. So all we had to do was get the taxi and tell the taxi driver what time to pick us up to go home; the job's a goodun!

I remember a teacher at school telling us the story of how St Andrew became the patron saint of Scotland. Apparently the place used to be known as Kilrymont until a Greek monk called St Rule was told by an angel to transport St Andrew's remains to the ends of the earth. He took them to Scotland and where he came ashore was called St Andrews. Apparently St Andrew is also the patron saint of many other places, including Greece, Russia and Amalfi. Anyway R.E. lesson over, we explored the town to find that their new fish and chip shop, Cromars, is almost as legendary as the famous golf course. It is a lovely golf course but all that bother about not letting women play there for years – did they not know Mary Queen of Scots played their links in 1567? In this day and age there should be no place for attitudes like that. There are a wide variety of shops in the town to suit every budget and every type of social event, be it a night out with friends, a student night out or a night out with royalty. The people are friendly and the town has a lovely ambience.

Day 4: St Andrews to Miltonhaven — 55 miles

We left St Andrews and drove to Miltonhaven Seaside Caravan Park and Campsite, just two miles north of St Cyrus. The weather wasn't the best but we stopped along the way for food and when we arrived on site it was raining hard. The site is quite small but right next to the coast and the owner has a few animals on site that young children love to see. When we

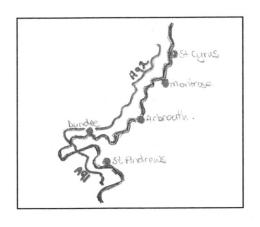

arrived we realised that we hadn't packed our assortment of DVDs for our night-time viewing if it's raining. I went to the shop to buy some milk and was talking to the owner who said it was going to be a long night unless we went out in waterproofs. I said we usually were stocked up with films to watch but had left them at home and he told me to pop back in 30 minutes. When I went back, he had raided his own collection and said just to drop the films in the next morning – what a kind man. The next morning before breakfast the sun was shining so we went for a walk along the beach which is quite stony but still pretty. We then had our breakfast outside which is always good. We had a plan for part of today. I had seen pictures of Dunnottar Castle and knew I wouldn't be able to drive past it without a visit. I love history. We didn't want to drive into Aberdeen but we could turn off towards Inverness after Dunnottar. We stopped at the car park and walked to the castle. It had been burnt to the ground a good few times by the Scottish to kill invading English armies. In the 10th century it was attacked by the Vikings. In 1297 it was captured by William Wallace. In 1562 it was visited by Mary Queen of Scots and in 1925 it was saved from ruin. So it has an extremely scary and blood-thirsty history. Rather disappointingly – it was closed. I would have to go back. When I saw the castle it made me think of a castle called Granmuir I had been reading about in *The Flower Reader*, a book by Elizabeth Loupas. Surely this was uncanny so I looked on my iPad and read that it is thought that she could have possibly based Granmuir in the story, on Dunnottar. I need to revisit when the castle is open but not on this trip. We turned and headed off to Inverness and our next pitch.

Day 5: Miltonhaven via Dunnottar to Inverness – 119 miles

We turned away from the east coast once we had been to Dunnottar and our next stop was going to be Inverness. I rang on ahead and booked us a pitch for that night. On the journey we passed through towns and villages which were all different and the countryside was green and rolling. As we approached Inverness the traffic got heavier and we felt like we were coming back into the world of busy people, a world we hadn't been part of for a few days. By now our food store was getting a bit empty so we drove straight through Inverness and on to the Bunchrew Caravan Park at Bunchrew. We discovered the campsite was about a 10 minute bus ride outside of town. The manager was very friendly and helpful, telling us if we needed to do any shopping where to catch the bus, get off, etc. The site itself was nicely positioned in relation to the town, with tree cover and open views overlooking the Beauly Firth. We set up on our pitch then went to wait for the bus just outside the gates to the site. When you have driven for a few hours it's a real treat to get the bus so we thought we would do some food shopping and treat ourselves to a meal out for tea. We were at the bus stop for about five minutes and a big school bus pulled in and gave us a lift into town. The driver said he was going to a school to take pupils home but picking us up and dropping us off before his job was no bother to him so we gave him our bus fares so at least he could treat himself to a tea, coffee or beer. When you're on a road trip its lovely because there are so many times when you get to see the very best in the people you meet.

Inverness is a lovely city and it is the most northerly one in

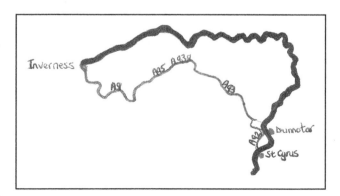

the UK, but I always think the High Street is often cold and windy. I remember hearing Billy Connolly once say in concert, "If a dog has a pee on Inverness High Street someone in Norway touches their cheek and says, 'It's raining.'" Joking aside, Inverness is a lovely city with every shop you could wish for, Primark, Debenhams and Marks and Spencer to name the important ones, as well as lots of lovely restaurants, cafés and pubs. There is also a great live music venue called the Ironworks where we once went to see the Tennessee Three, who were Johnny Cash's original backing band. I guarantee boredom is not an option here.

We did our food shopping, grabbed something nice to eat in a pub on the High Street, then caught the bus back to the site. We then got our comfy Hobbit chairs out and sat facing the setting sun and watching the water, chatting over the day's events, talking with groups of friendly German and Dutch people on holiday who were barbecuing and drinking wine. Everyone was friendly and enjoying their holiday. As it got later, everyone headed into their vans to rest, watch the TV or, in our case, to plan tomorrow's adventure.

Day 6 and 7: Inverness to Fortrose – 14 miles

We didn't rush to get up because we didn't have a long drive today as we were headed for the Black Isle, which conjures up all manner of mystery and dark deeds. In actual fact it's really called the Black Isle due to the colour of the soil I believe. The Black Isle is beautiful as was the weather, not too hot but perfect for me – a redhead with freckles who turns into an itchy red mess in the heat. We were headed to Fortrose Bay Campsite just beside the golf course. The pitches are right next to the beach where the Beauly Firth meets the Moray Firth. This is where the sea laps, a beautiful sound, about 10 feet away from the van, only separated by a strip of sandy beach and it soothes you to sleep. This is where people walk down to where the sea and river meet as each tide turns every day, to see the dolphins showing off as well as the passing seals who do not like to be outdone. All of this takes place about seven feet away from where you're standing which is a real pain to try to catch on camera because you never get that shot you want. They are so close you can almost touch them; they will clear the water holding a salmon in their mouth and you will find that

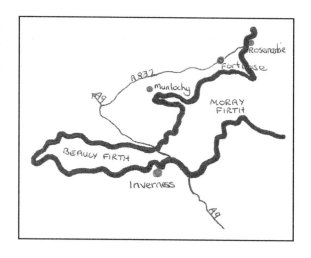

your camera is being temperamental and you miss the shot. There are the stalwarts who stand there for hours with every type of photographic equipment but even they can be bitterly disappointed with their results. Those cheeky dolphins and seals know how to make you miss that lovely shot; they have had so much practice and laugh their fins off as they dive under, leaving your camera jammed and another opportunity missed. I say – forget the camera; you will never forget that feeling of excitement when you see your first dolphin or seal. They look at you and tease you – resist the urge to take that photo.

From Chanonry Point, where the dolphins hold centre stage, you can walk along the beach to another beautiful place called Rosemarkie. The Rosemarkie Bay Beach Café on the beach is run by the local people and they serve a good pot of tea or coffee. They always give you a card for your next free cuppa as well. In the town itself there are an assortment of shops and a museum where you can see Pictish symbol stones dating back to the 8th century if you feel inclined. I popped into a shop called Panacea to see Cornelia, a homeopath. She sells a wide variety of spiritual and well-being items. I have a skin complaint and she makes me up a pot of ointment. She is the calmest and most peaceful and pleasant lady I have ever met, always ready at the end of the internet if you need advice.

I don't think I mentioned that the Black Isle is in fact a peninsula and from Rosemarkie you can catch a bus to the far end of the peninsula. The town of Cromarty is right at the end and when you get off the bus you can see the old oil rigs abandoned in the water, all monuments to a bygone era. They are all being decommissioned. In the town itself there are cafés, pubs and a few shops. It's an interesting place to explore. We had a look around then went for a cuppa and, by the time we got to the bus stop, there was a bus due to leave for Fortrose.

It's well worth a visit and it's great getting a double decker because we go upstairs and sit in the front seats. I must admit it was a bit of a hair-raising ride as there are lots of sharp bends and one or two tall trees brushing the windows. Before we continued our journey there was one more place we wanted to visit – the Clootie Well near the village of Munlochy – a place shrouded in mystery and magic. The A832 runs alongside the car park.

The Clootie Well is a healing well and belongs to an ancient tradition that was once common practice in Scotland and Ireland. Some people have said that the well was originally the house of a fairy to whom a gift of cloth had to be given before the pilgrim could drink the health-giving and luck-bestowing water. The well was adopted into the Christian religion and became known as St Boniface's (or Curitan's) Well, who worked as a missionary in Scotland around AD620. In those days pilgrims would come to the well and perform a ceremony that involved circling the well three times in the direction the sun takes across the sky every day before splashing water from the well on the ground and saying a prayer. If they were praying for someone else who was ill, they would then tie a piece of cloth that had been in contact with the person to a nearby tree. If they were there for healing themselves they would tie a piece of material that had been in contact with the sore body part. So, if someone had a hand injury, they would leave a glove to rot on the tree, the idea being that as the material rotted away, so would the illness. In days gone by sick children would have been left alone there overnight to be healed. The whole place is really creepy in day time so I can't ever imagine being left there alone in the dark.

The car park itself is eerily quiet and not a place you would want to stay in for long. Sounds seem muffled as well, don't ask me why, but there's an atmosphere; good or bad – it's hard to tell. You walk from the car park and into the forest where you are suddenly surrounded by all manner of garments, scarves or material hanging from the trees. The only problem now is that a lot of the materials do not rot but hang buffeted and torn to shreds by the weather. Some look like they have been there for years, a ragged display of hopes and fashions through the years. It's a strange place, I think, awesome in the thought-provoking-but-with-an-air-of-fear-and-respect, meaning of the word. It was interesting to see but I found the place oppressive in a strange way and it felt good to get out of the woods, into the van and back on to the road.

Day 8: Munlochy to Wick – 104 miles

We were heading for Wick, a former Viking settlement in earlier times, "Vik" in Viking meaning "bay". Apparently they used Wick harbour for their long ships. We had another fine day and we realised we knew nothing much about Wick at all. In fact we drove through a lot of places on the A9 before turning on to the A99 to get there, all of which were interesting and worth a peep.

We decided we would find our site first then spend the rest of the day exploring on foot. The Wick Caravan and Camping Site is right in the centre of town, down on the river. It was a very steep drive in and the same steep drive out, but the site was really well maintained by a very nice kindly warden and was very pleasant. Wick itself has history in the herring fishing industry since 1790. In the 1860s, for 12 weeks during the summer, the population of 6000 used to increase to 15,000 when migrant workers came in to help process, pack the fish and mend the nets. Herring fishing was in steep decline by the 1930s. The discovery of North Sea Oil has added to the local economy and there is an airport at Wick. We walked up into town and the first thing we saw was the shortest street in the world, Ebenezer Place, built in 1883. It is just 2.06 metres or 6 feet 9 inches in length. It makes up one end of the Makays Hotel. Wick is definitely worth a good look around.

Day 9: Wick to Dunnet Bay – 19 miles

Next on our route was John O'Groats, a place that takes its name from Jan de Groot, a Dutch immigrant who ran the ferry to Orkney (I bet getting on that ferry was a blast in those days). He built a house in the 1480s in an octagonal shape with eight windows and eight doors for himself and each of his seven quarrelsome sons to use. They all sat round an octagonal table so no one could be at the head of the table. There's no mention of his poor wife; maybe after giving birth to seven sons she might have escaped through one of those doors and never looked back.

I was quite excited because my Dad had told me about some of his cyclist friends who had cycled from there to Lands End and vice versa. As we drove in, it seemed to be a very spread-out town, with a good few gift shops and the famous sign post where everyone wants their photograph taken, being the place everyone headed for. I was horrified to see that you had to pay to have your photo taken at the proper sign and that the place names were missing from the sign. We spoke to cyclists we had seen on the road earlier and took photos for them, but I found it hard to imagine pedalling all that way and not being able to

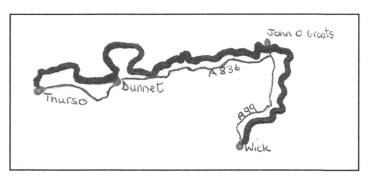

take a photo yourself with all the place names on and instead having to ring a number for the sign to be put in place. We saw the ferry heading to Orkney but I wasn't tempted; it looked a tad on the choppy side for me, so we looked around, had our lunch and a cuppa then continued our journey.

We were booked at Dunnet Bay Caravan Club Site. The site was very good with plenty of amenities and very caring staff who were very proud of their site and who were more than happy to tell you what to see while you were there. The views from the site were breathtaking. The beach of golden sand was backed by big dunes. There were surfer dudes taking their chances on the big waves, I never expected it to be like this – a scene from Point Break. We thoroughly enjoyed our surroundings and felt invigorated. We decided to check out Thurso while we were in that area. Apparently it has the most northerly railway station. They call it the Far North Line – if it was any further north, it would be an underwater station in the Pentland Firth. But seriously, Thurso is a lovely town to visit with shops, cafés and a museum, oh, and there's a surfing shop in the harbour.

Day 10, 11 and 12: Dunnet Bay to Durness – 80 miles

We drove from Dunnet Bay along the A836, in my favourite type of weather – fine but not hot. We passed Dounreay, the nuclear power station, and noticed there are some lovely bays and interesting places en route with names like Coldbackie and Tongue. The road itself is narrow with passing places; it meanders through rocky moorland which tends to be largely uninhabited. At the Kyle of Tongue we drove across

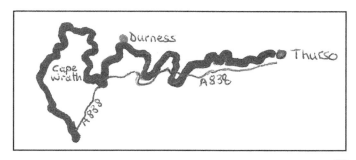

the bridge. I will be surprised at anyone who fails to register the beauty of this place. There is a story of how Bonnie Prince Charlie's Jacobite rebellion in 1746 was affected by events that happened when the ship, the Hazard, carrying £13,000 in gold from France was intercepted by the Royal Navy frigate HMS Sheerness. The men escaped off the ship with the gold, planning to carry it overland but were intercepted by the McKay clan. In a desperate attempt, the crew threw the gold coins into the loch. When Bonny Prince Charlie heard of this, he sent 1500 of his men to try to get the gold from the loch, but they were defeated on the way there. Some historians say that had these men been fighting with him at Culloden, history might have been very different. The money was later recovered by the government but there have been tales of cattle still coming out of the mud with a gold coin stuck in their hoof. History lesson done, we continued driving along the road following the shores of Loch Eribol. As we approached a sign for Smoo Cave we decided to have a look because you can walk to it down the wooden stairs from the car park off the A838. Smoo Cave got its name from the old Norse word 'Smuga', which means 'hiding place'. It is a massive natural sea cave carved into limestone cliffs, well worth a look, or even a trip into, if you have time. There is an opportunity for people to write their names or messages on the hillside using stones and pebbles from the beach and anyone can join in the tradition. There are many stories linked with Smoo Cave. For years some people said it was the residence of the devil. In 1814, when he was cruising around Scotland, Sir Walter Scott said of Smoo Cave, "A water kelpie or evil spirit of aquatic propensities could not have chosen a fitter abode." After all the 107 steps you never noticed on the way down to see the cave, the word "fitter" flashes in neon in your brain as you walk back to the top. Smoo itself used to be an RAF station and you can wander around the old buildings. Surprisingly, there is a community garden dedicated to John Lennon who used to come to Durness for his holidays with his family.

It was afternoon when we drove into Durness and saw our campsite. We were amazed. It was set out on the headland looking out to sea and our pitch was the perfect one. We were booked at the Sango Sands Oasis for two nights. In Northumberland, where we live, the beaches are legendary for their beauty, but Sango Sands took my breath away. The pitch was on the headland overlooking the beach which was a long way down; there was a wooden walkway that took you to the farthest point way out in the bay. I'm sure other people who have been there will vouch for me when I say the sea was light turquoise and the tips of the waves were dazzling white. Next to home, it was the most beautiful place I have ever seen. The next day our plan was to visit Cape Wrath.

Cape Wrath (side trip on Day 11)

We knew absolutely nothing about Cape Wrath other than it is the most north-westerly point on the Scottish mainland and everyone on the site had either been or wanted to go, so we asked the warden about the trip and he told us that if we wanted to actually get there the next day, we would have to go to the pier at Keoldale, where you get the boat across to Cape Wrath, by 8 am. So I was "up the night before." I take after my Grandad Dick, who always liked to be early and could be totally relied on to get you to wherever you wanted to be on time. We parked up and noticed we were about eighth and ninth in the queue. I spoke to a German man who had tried to go there for three years and each time there were too many people in front of him. He was in front of us so we were hoping his luck held out. There is no other way to access it for the public so you have to get on the Cape Wrath Ferry which is little more than a big rowing boat with an engine on, holding about 16 people. It takes about 10 minutes to cross the Kyle of Durness. I think they make the trip twice a day depending on the tides and when you arrive you transfer on to a mini bus which is waiting for you. You then have a rough ride with a driver's very interesting commentary telling you how Cape Wrath is a site of special scientific interest as well as a special protection area for birds. You travel over wild moorland to the lighthouse. The buses don't go fast but it feels fast due to the terrain. The wildlife you see is fantastic, as is the whole experience.

Cape Wrath is still used by the Ministry of Defence for military training and is sometimes closed to the public. Also, nearby Garvie Island is used for bombing practice. When you arrive at the lighthouse you can see where the west coast meets the north and the views are stunning. The Atlantic stretches out in front of you and the wild moorland is behind you. There are no more land masses between here and the Arctic. The Clo Mor Cliffs are the highest in Britain at 281 metres or, for those of you like me who prefer Imperial measurements, it's 921 feet. They are sheer and there are lots of different sea birds to see. There is a café called the Ozone Cafe run by a husband and wife who are lovely and who can tell you lots of information. You should read their own story about the Christmas Turkey. There is so much I could tell you about Cape Wrath because everything about it is fantastic, a true nature lovers getaway, breathtaking in every respect from the bumps you drive over to those amazing cliffs. On the journey everything in and around you rattles, but it's a trip not to be missed – so I would say a rattling good trip.

Day 13: Durness to Ullapool – 68 miles

It was raining quite heavily when we left Durness but, by the time we stopped for a cuppa at Scourie Bay, the sun was coming out. We parked beside a bird hide, made our drink then sat in the hide watching the birds on the deserted beach. I made a mental note of coming back to this beautiful white sand beach with turquoise water sometime in the future. As we left Scourie I remembered one of my friends had told me we had to see Lochinver so I asked Jim if we could take a right turn and drive to Lochinver for lunch. The town itself is in Assynt, on the west coast of Scotland and built along the shores of Loch Inver. Fishing seems to be an important industry here as I noticed quite a few boats, but I might be wrong; maybe they were for tourist trips. We did see a few wild life sea cruises advertised. We also saw quite a few walkers and people with climbing gear. We went to the An Cala Cafe and Bunkhouse. As we sat down I noticed that the table cloths were made in the unmistakable black and white check of the Northumbrian tartan so when we ordered lunch, it came as a great surprise to hear our own Geordie accent. The lady who took our order came from South Shields. Who would have bet on that happening? As we were eating we saw a lady who I said we had seen on telly. We were both trying to look without being obvious

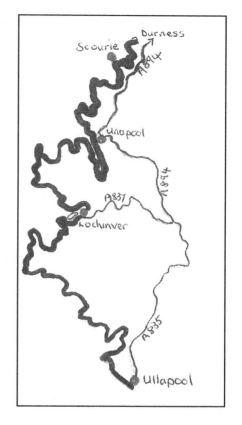

but by the time we realised who she was she was leaving. It was none other than the actress, Sheila Hancock.

We left Lochinver and got back on the road to Ullapool. We had booked to stay at the Broomfield Holiday Park, which is right in the centre of Ullapool and handy for everything as we needed to stock up on food again. I was ready for a fix of shops and mooching around where there were people. We parked up and we had a free view of the ferry going out to Lewis. I looked at the choppy water further out and wondered could I have got on the ferry to face the four-hour journey and I quietly thought, "not today gladiator." For Jim that would have been no problem, but he is perfectly happy to take me to Lewis and Harris on another trip from Uig on Skye where, I found out from our map, the journey is much shorter. Today we decided to shop.

Ullapool is large town and is popular with tourists. It lies on Loch Broom. The North Atlantic Drift that you probably learned about in geography passes by Ullapool and moderates the temperature. It was too hot for me; I needed the thermostat to be moderated a bit lower. The harbour is a port for fishing, yachting and the ferry to Stornaway. It's a centre famous for music and the arts. In October there's a guitar festival and the Loopallu Festival is world famous attracting 2500 people from all over the world. There are lots of places to eat, drink and be merry and the people are very friendly. We got stocked up the next morning at the supermarket, filled the tank with petrol and in glorious sunshine headed off to Gairloch, our next place.

Day 14 and 15: Ullapool to Gairloch — 56 miles

I don't want to bore anyone, but the scenery on the way to Gairloch is amazing and we revelled in it. Any water we saw was sparkling bright blue and we could see for miles. Unfortunately for me it was too hot and rashes were starting up on both legs; in hot weather it gets miserable but I have my creams and potions. We had booked a site at the Gairloch

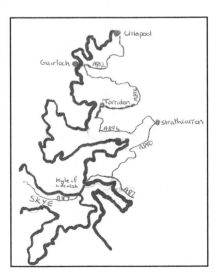

Caravan Park, which overlooks Gairloch Bay and we felt blessed to be able to see such beauty. We felt at one with nature; this is God's country and I felt we are "truly taking time to do what makes our souls happy," to use someone else's quote that so perfectly matched our mood. I had never really noticed so much sparklingly blue sea and deserted golden beaches stretching for so far I couldn't even guess. We walked from the site into the town and noticed a host of really special shops: a bookshop that had a café, restaurants, pubs and gift shops and even a radio station. It was very hot and we were the only people around; it seemed like siesta time where everything is quiet. We wandered along the beach, mooched in the shops for shade, then headed back to sit and cook some food. There is so much you can do here, like take a boat trip to see the wildlife in the sea or walk to see wildlife in the mountains or woodland. We found a hill walk just along the road from our campsite and walked there as the sun was going down. The views across the bay and surrounding area were magnificent and impossible to describe in words for a pleb like me. My English teacher always told me I would make a good foreigner and once asked me where I had learned English. It hurt me at the time because she was seriously annoyed – I was only 13 and was so embarrassed. But, in a way, she was right because I am a languages teacher who has always loved languages. Seriously, Gairloch is a place not to be missed. From there we decided to check out the Isle of Skye.

Day 16 and 17: Gairloch to Portree – 101 miles

We left Gairloch in sunshine on the A832; we stopped at Talladale and decided we would like to stay at the Loch Maree Hotel sometime. The views from the rooms must be amazing but the trees and mountains surrounding the area make it all the more beautiful. We passed the Beinn Eighe Visitor Centre, but we had quite a drive so we kept going and turned on to the A896 to Torridon where we stopped for a sandwich and a cuppa. The area is mountainous and wooded. We didn't stop long because there were one or two midges. We drove to Shieldaig and on to the A87 to Portree. We were booked on a site just outside Portree, the Torvaig Caravan

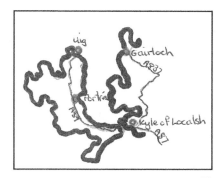

and Campsite. We stopped in the town for food shopping and saw lots of midge nets for sale – we should have kept driving. The campsite was near the coast but there were millions of midges. It was impossible to go out after 7:30 pm without them attacking your head kamikaze style, in droves. We were stuck in the van because we didn't have midge stuff and Skye midges don't take prisoners. On Skye in summer, the nights are light for much longer than they are in Newcastle so it was light until long after midnight. The next day we decided to go to Dunvegan, which is the seat of the McCleods. My Nan was born Annie McCloud and I wanted to go and see where the Scottish branch of my family had lived. We caught the bus and that was a real treat. When we arrived in Dunvegan we walked around then went to the beach and saw seals lounging on the rocks, at close quarters. It was a lovely day and the people we met were really friendly and helpful. Now it was back to the van, but tonight we were ready for the midges. We had discovered that Jim was a midge's delight while "thankfully" I wasn't quite so juicy. We were ready; we had the gear – 'Skin so Soft' and 'Smidge' (used by the SAS) and a couple of midge nets to wear – but that night it was breezy so we hardly saw the little buggers. That night we enjoyed the evening sitting outside, while we planned our next journey to Fort William

Day 18: Portree to Fort William – 108 miles (via ferry from Armadale)

We drove from Portree, heading for Armadale. We had decided we

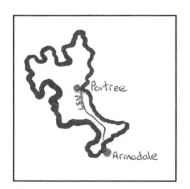

would take the ferry to Mallaig which meant we could take in the "Road to the Isles", the A830 Mallaig to Fort William which, in our case, was the "Road Away from the Isles". Scotland's most famous West Highland railway journey from Glasgow via Fort William to Mallaig is among the world's most beautiful and scenic journeys. It is also famous, more recently, due to the Harry Potter film where the train is seen crossing the 21-arched Glenfinnan Viaduct. We thought it might be beautiful by road as there are places where the railway runs close to the road and people stand on the bridges to see the Jacobite Steam Train

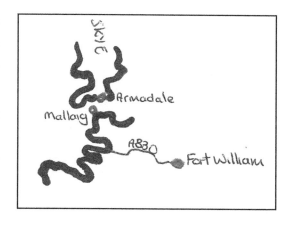

go by. The drive more than lived up to our expectations. All the places are beautiful: Morar, with its beaches of silver sand, which I learned was made famous in the film *Local Hero* and where there is, reputedly, another monster called Morag who lives in Loch Morar which is deeper than Loch Ness; Arisaig where the Arisaig Highland Games are held every year in July and Glenfinnan where Bonnie Prince Charlie started the Jacobite rebellion in 1745. There is a column on the spot to mark the occasion and the Glenfinnan Visitors Centre, which is well worth a visit.

We arrived in Fort William early evening and made straight for the Glen Nevis Caravan and Camping Park, which was bathed in warm sunshine and where we had fantastic views of Ben Nevis. For the first time in years we saw the top. My husband pointed out the walking route he and his friend had taken a few years earlier. We set up shop, ready to cook and then I realised I had forgotten to get milk, tea bags and sugar and without those I knew I would be miserable. Because it had been a busy day and the shop on the site was now closed we decided to ring a local taxi firm and asked would they take us to the nearest shop. We had no idea how far away from the town we were as there weren't many people around to ask. The taxi arrived and took us round the corner to a big garage where they sold everything and charged us £5 for the privilege. We had to laugh – we must have been away 10 minutes and 6 of those we must have been waiting in the queue. We made damn sure we enjoyed that cuppa and had a good laugh. The next day when we got sorted and, after we were packed, it was business as usual. We were headed for Oban to catch the ferry to Mull. I had rung on ahead to our favourite site at Craignure and requested a pitch facing the sea.

Day 19: Fort William to Oban – 44 miles

Fort William is the end of the West Highland Way and we saw lots of happy people finishing their walk all the way from Milngavie, just outside of Glasgow, as we drove out on the A82, again through beautiful scenery.

I always wish that I could do a long walk; my best friend walked the West Highland Way and was so chuffed when she finished but she did say the midges lay in wait at certain parts of the walk, so defensive tactics were needed. For a few years now I have thought about the Camino which starts in France and goes across the Pyrenees into Spain, finishing in Galicia at Santiago de Compostela. I was once fortunate enough to go there on an intensive language course and it was such an interesting and beautiful place. But the thing is, I enjoy walking but not to the extent where I hurt and I am a very plain eater so in Spain my staple diet would either be plain rice, pasta or potatoes with plain chicken, so that has always curbed my enthusiasm. Then, of course, you have to consider the choice of clothing – you know what a poor packer I am already. I would be the one with the donkey carrying all my bags. Seriously though, I have

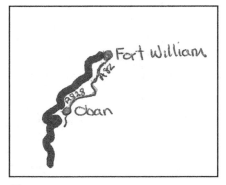

nothing but admiration for people who take on any walking challenge. Maybe it's just not for me or maybe once I take that first step and try a stage I might get hooked. We could consider driving to the Camino in Ruby. I can see another book title,"Ruby gets her Compostela" Just an idea.

En route to Oban, if at all possible, I wanted to look at the Corran Ferry which links the Morvern and the Ardnamurchan peninsula as I had read how beautiful the scenery was there and we had an idea of visiting it on another trip. We drove past Loch Creran where a few years earlier we had booked the most amazing house with our family one New Year. The house had a glass front with views across the loch; it had its own beach and we spent a magical New Year there with a fire on the beach, fireworks and lanterns.

Day 19 and 20: Oban to Craignure (Isle of Mull) – 28 miles

Eventually we got to Oban, in time for our ferry, sat on deck and waited to see if any dolphins would welcome us on the journey over. They did, four of them jumping out of the water ahead and to the right of the boat. There was a man standing with a massive camera on one side of the boat and yes, you have already guessed – he missed them because he was facing the wrong way. It was so funny. The journey was smooth and soon we were at the Shieling Holidays site in Craignure. The staff at the campsite are so helpful and friendly and are always happy to tell you news about the site. They have a blackboard in the office telling you of the wildlife people have seen on site or in the area. We parked up and then went exploring the town to look for an evening meal which we had at the local pub right next to the site. The food there was good and after a post-dinner walk we went back to plan our next day's activities sitting under a bright starry sky.

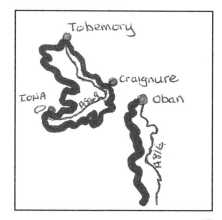

We drove from there to Fionnport. The weather was glorious – sunny but chilly. We had decided to get the ferry to Iona which is for pedestrians only and very small, but then the crossing isn't far. I have to say again the beauty of the place is overwhelming. The sand on the beach is white and the sea is turquoise. People go there to see where St Columba worked and it is a place where people go for spiritual retreats. It is so peaceful but gets very busy during the day. We went into the abbey and there were three ladies from Holland who performed an impromptu Taizé chant which sounded beautiful in the surroundings. We climbed Dun I the highest point on the island. It was a clear sunny day and we could see for miles. If you want to eat on Iona, I suggest finding somewhere straight away when you arrive because the cafés, pubs and restaurants are extremely popular and soon fill up. Alternatively, if you prefer, it's a perfect idea to take your own food, find a bench to sit on and picnic, admiring the views while you munch. We were booked on to Fidden Farm that night, right next to Iona but back on Mull. I don't know if you can camp on Iona but I think if you can it must be an uplifting experience. We had no idea what Fidden Farm was like, but it has to be one thing you do if you have a camper van or tent. You rock up, pay for your pitch then pick wherever you like. There are no hook ups so it's wild camping. Our pitch had an open view of the sea and the small beach cove in front of us. It was a bit like a lagoon in front of you. The sand is white and the sea is turquoise and you can see to the bottom. That night there was a full moon and the sand on the bottom of the pool was reflecting the light. This was one of our happiest places – so unbelievably beautiful and will be etched in our minds forever. Just Jim, me, the moonlight and Ruby. We stayed for two nights then hit the trail back to Craignure for the ferry to Oban. There are so many things I could tell you about Mull, like the dolphins who seem to welcome and say goodbye to all the visitors; the golden eagle we saw just above our van; the brightly coloured houses of Tobermory. There we spoke to a young lad from Brisbane who was touring the UK on a bike with his dog sitting in a truck he was towing. We also met two ponies who were jealous of each other. When Jim patted them, one insisted on an extra pat and the other one kicked it, before they both went in a huff to opposite ends of the field. I reckon once you have been to Mull you will never tire of returning.

Day 21: Craignure to Oban, then Tayinloan — 69 miles

Oban lay ahead of us as did our next trip. It was going to be Isla and Kintyre. We needed to plan where first. We choose our places as the mood takes us. We always make our minds up on the way. It all adds to the sense of freedom you have in a van. Whoever said, "Travel as far as you can, as much as you can, as long as you can. Life's not meant to be lived in one place," knew what they were talking about. For Jim and me the journey and the places are equally exciting, so we headed for the A816 and the destination was Tayinloan on the Kintyre peninsula.

The drive from Oban to Tayinloan is scenic and also quite busy. Our plan was to enjoy the drive. We had stayed in Kilmelford one New Year with family and felt nostalgic as we passed the pub, thinking of all the fun we had had at the Ceilidh that night. Our plan was to stop at Kilmartin taking in the stone circles and cairns. I have never seen so many in one place. This is the most important prehistoric site in Scotland. I won't try to explain them and what they tell us; all I can say is they are amazing and it's like looking through a window into history, which cannot fail to reach your imagination. From the Temple Wood Stone Circle we walked to Kilmartin Church where you can see very old grave stones and crosses. There is also a Museum of Ancient Culture, but we didn't have time to visit. After a cuppa it was back to Ruby and on to the road the A83. We stopped in Lochgilpead to stock up on food and,

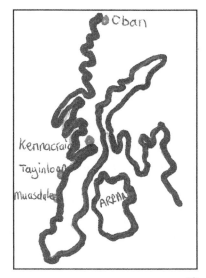

for a future trip, checked out the site in the centre of town; it was big and busy but seemed fine. We reached the Kintyre peninsula and, as we were nearing Tayinloan, we saw an awful accident. I don't think I have mentioned any roads other than to say they were single track, but the A83 is a very smooth road; I might have said it would be a great one to roller skate on when I was about ten years old and I think people tend to drive quite fast in places, or it seemed like that to us. Someone had tried to avoid another car on a tight bend and had gone off the road, almost overturned and was in the trees at the side of the road. After seeing that we were wary of oncoming traffic and were pleased when we reached our destination. The Point Sands Holiday Park is among my favourites. It has everything you need and is a friendly site. Our pitch overlooked a white sand beach covered with scallop shells – the sign of the pilgrim. I picked one up and kept it for the van. We felt like pilgrims on a journey and to use a part of Mark Nepo's quote, "To journey and be transformed by the journey is to be a pilgrim." The sun was shining across Isla, the Paps of Jura and Gigha as we sat on the beach. It was 9:30 pm in the evening and some people had lit a fire on the beach and another group to our left were barbecuing. This was bliss. It was still warm but more importantly there wasn't a midge in sight. We sat till it got as dark as it gets out west, then sat at our hobbit table on our hobbit chairs planning our next visit.

Day 22: Tayinloan to Gigha, then Muasdale – 4 miles

There was no rush to get on the road today as we only had a short drive. We were booked on a site in Muasdale, but decided to explore Gigha. We decided to leave Ruby parked at the ferry and travel across as pedestrians. The crossing is very short. After only 20 minutes you find yourself in Ardminish, the only village on the island. I have to say at this point, we only explored the village and walked a little way out then deposited ourselves in the Boathouse bar and café by the pier. They also have pitches here for campers and camper vans which are right next to the beach. It seemed lovely but we were sorted for the night so we enjoyed our food and drinks then headed back to the ferry and Muasdale.

The Muasdale Holiday Park is beautifully located, with fantastic beach views and it is spotless. The couple who run the site are really friendly, kind and helpful and cater for everyone's needs. Everything was spot on and they deserved six stars for their thoughtfulness and hard work. We explored the area and were bowled over by the views as we walked along, deciding on our next plan. Because we were so near, we decided to take in Islay by driving to Kennacraig and getting the ferry to Port Ellen.

Day 23, 24 and 25: Muasdale to Kennacraig and ferry to Islay – 17 miles

We knew nothing about Islay other than when we booked they pronounce it Isla, so we started saying that as well. We had been told by a man as we drove into the car park for the ferry that Islay was the Queen of the Hebrides. That was news to us. In fact we knew very little about Islay and the saying ,"Once a year go someplace you've never been before" sprang to mind. We boarded the ferry at Kennacraig for the two hour journey. Before we did I asked a man who had just disembarked if it was a rough crossing but he said "No", today was a smooth crossing. We were sailing to Port Ellen. The journey itself was pleasant. We had breakfast then wandered around the boat and outside to take photos. When we arrived on the island, to our right I think I saw every name of whisky distillery: Laphroaig, Lagavulin and Ardbeg (and I am teetotal, just in case you are wondering). But I always like to look at the bottles to see how unusual some of them are, that's all. I didn't know what the island was like or really anything about it other than Walter Campbell,

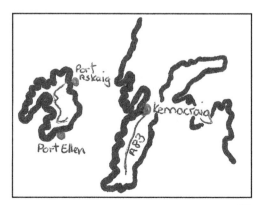

who planned the town Port Ellen in 1821, had named it after his wife Eleanor, which I thought was a nice thing to do. The Carraig Fhada Lighthouse in the bay, which is an unusual shape, was also erected in her memory – so she must have been a really special lady.

Our site was in Port Charlotte, a community run site at Port Mòr, so we drove through Bowmore, which is a busy town with a good few shops and is dominated by a big round church at the top of a steep hill in the centre of the town. It's round because whoever built it said that the devil would have nowhere to hide. The Tartan Pimpernel, Donald Caskie, who helped more than 2000 allied servicemen to escape from France during the Second World War, was born in Bowmore – another interesting fact I never knew. We stocked up on provisions at the big Co-op supermarket then headed on to Port Charlotte. As we were driving along, people on the other side of the road were waving their hands at us. At first I thought something was wrong with the van, but when we arrived I asked the man on the site and he says everyone on the island does that to acknowledge good driving all the time and every day. We arrived on site and our pitch surpassed all our expectations. We had a sea view and plenty of space and privacy and the people on site couldn't have been nicer. There was a lovely café/restaurant run by the community which did breakfasts, lunches and evening meals with the lovely views – what more could you want? We spent time on site chilling out. The next day we explored the Museum of Islay Life in Port Charlotte, which was really interesting and enjoyable. Then we drove to Portnahaven, Port Wemyss, Kilchiaren and ended up at Kilchoman Bay which was wild and windy with fantastic waves. It was a grey drizzly day and the sea was grey, topped with massive white waves. We could hear the waves crashing in the bay from the van and we were on a road above the beach. I had read that there is a sailor's cemetery nearby with 75 graves of the 400 sailors who drowned when an armed merchant cruiser the SS Otranto collided with another ship in its convoy in 1918. Of the 400 men who had to swim ashore, only 16 survived. There's another memorial at Sanaigmore commemorating 241 Irish Immigrants who drowned when fleeing the Irish potato famine in April 1847 – a reminder of how treacherous this beautiful coastline was and still is.

We stayed on Islay for three days and on our second day, which dawned bright and sunny, we decided to visit Finlaggan, the headquarters of the Lords of the Isles since the 12th century. You have to walk along duck boards over reed beds to gain access. There are a couple of prehistoric crannogs (artificial islands) and the main crannog is called Eilean Mor. This used to be connected to a smaller crannog via a causeway where the lords had their meetings. There is an information centre which we found interesting and fills in any information gaps you might have. If crannog life is something that fascinates you, I recommend the crannog at Aberfeldy on the mainland, where you can experience the way of life in those times, for instance, the types of food they ate and making a fire using wooden sticks. The Finlaggan area is truly beautiful and we enjoyed our drive back to Port Charlotte. We knew we had to be up early the next morning for the 6 am Ferry from Port Askaig, so we would be travelling up this road again before taking the ferry back to Kennacraig.

Day 26: Kennacraig to Claonaig and ferry to Lochranza – 5 miles

We had a very smooth early morning crossing on what was looking to be another fine day. We arrived in Kennacraig and were going to Claonaig to get the ferry to Lochranza on the isle of Arran. Claonaig is a very small ferry port and the road from Kennacraig takes you straight on to the ferry. This ferry is quite small, the type where you drive your car or van on to the middle of the boat then you can sit in your van or take the steps either side of the boat to a deck where you can stand or sit. If it's a windy day you feel like Jack Sparrow in the film, *Pirates of the Caribbean*. The crossing takes about 50 minutes and it's quite long enough on that type of boat, believe me, for someone who hasn't got the stomach of a sea

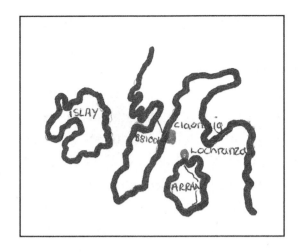

dog. As we boarded the ferry a small party of cyclists were propping their bikes near to the van and one cyclist stood back to let me walk up the stairs. As I thanked him I wondered how I knew him. I knew his face but couldn't place him at all and didn't want to stare. I told Jim I had seen someone but was at a loss as to how or where I knew him from. Fifteen minutes later I said to Jim, "I know who he is, it's Ali McCoist." Jim had no idea who or what I was talking about but we turned around and he was speaking to the crew. Jim confirmed my identification as correct then laughed at me when I told Jim that his bike was right next to my side of the van and I was going to ask for a selfie. I had seen him on TV on A Question of Sport; he had played football for Sunderland, then Rangers and became the Rangers manager when he retired from playing. Jim shook his head and laughed and said he was getting into the van; he totally disowned me. I went over to say "hello" and Ali McCoist said how much he had missed a Geordie accent and how much he had loved playing football in our region. When I asked for a photo he gave my phone to one of his friends who was taking part in the charity ride with him. I told him my husband had disowned me and pointed to him, Ali went across and they chatted like long lost friends about his footballing career. He was so sociable and after I had dared to speak to him everyone else wanted pictures and he was happy to oblige. He was doing the Five Ferries Cycle Route of 72 miles, a special cycle ride taking in some of the islands as well. What a lovely person he was to meet. I could now add him to my list of famous people, along with Heather Myles (country singer), Bonnie Raitt (Blues) and Eve Sellis (country singer). I was on a high when we arrived at Lochranza. It was early in the morning so we had a day ahead to explore Arran. We decided to sightsee before checking in to the site later on in the day. Arran is famous for tourism and has seven golf courses. I made a mental note to tell my brother who is a lifelong passionate golfer. When we stopped for coffee we met a couple of geology students who were enthusing about the rocks. I didn't bother getting the details but they were excited. The capital is Brodick where the ferry terminal is. It's set on a wide bay and its shops are spread out on the main road around the bay. There's Arran Aromatics where you can buy wonderful creams and potions as well as candles and other gifts and beside there is the Islands Cheese Company where you can get a wide variety of special cheeses made on Arran. Both places are well worth a visit. There's also Brodick Castle with its walled garden, but we have never been there. I have saved it for another visit. Goatfell, 2866 feet high, towers over Brodick and is accessible in three hours from Brodick, but I'm no Chris Bonington and I've never felt the urge to climb anything as high as that. The views must be fantastic but I'm happy to believe people who tell me about it. We explored Brodick and drove through some lovely seaside places like Sannox and Corrie, then went back to check into the Lochranza Campsite early afternoon.

We stopped at the office to find out about our pitch. The warden took us down, but when we got there I asked if we could have a different pitch because it was too near the trees which, in Scotland, means the possibility of midges. He gave us a much better pitch, so we parked up and decided to explore around Lochranza itself. We saw the deer on the beach near to the ruined castle on the mud flats and on the golf course totally unperturbed by our presence. Then we headed back to our site. It was about 5:30 pm and the sight that met our eyes filled us both with dread – everyone was wearing midge nets – the place was swarming with them. Jim's heart sank because he knew that they saw him as a feast on legs. I went into the shop and bought us each a midge net as we had lost the two we bought on Skye – a pink one for me and a black one for Jim (I know how to spoil a man). "Don't say I never treat you to something new," I said as I gave Jim his. Then I rummaged in the van for the Smidge and the Skin so Soft. Midges hate both Smidge and Skin so Soft and if you have a small fan in your van to switch on, they keep out – but there's always the cheeky hundred ready to risk annihilation. You soon pick up the art of eating under a net. I decided to choose six ways to wear a midge net for my friends on Facebook which caused a lot of hilarity. It can be arranged very fetchingly if image is important to you.

Day 27: Lochranza to Kildonan – 27 miles

But seriously, in spite of the Lochranza site being a lovely friendly site with a good location, we were at the starting blocks the next morning to drive to Seal Shore Campsite at Kildonan where Maurice and his daughter Theresa keep a beautifully clean, usually midge-free site. I had rang Maurice the previous evening and explained our dilemma. He had a pitch but no hook up so we would be wild camping. As long as it wasn't chilly we would be fine. On another occasion, when we had booked, we arrived there to find our pitch was almost on the beach. It couldn't have been better. Unfortunately for us, within five minutes of arriving there, I had locked us out of the van and everything we needed –

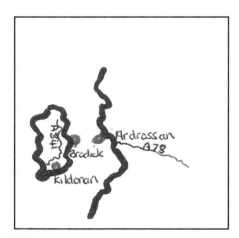

phone, RAC card – was inside. I told Maurice who just sorted everything out for us, calmed me down and rang the RAC. It was two and a half hours later when a kindly man from Brodick had managed to sort out the problem. It took him all of five minutes. This is why Seal Shore is always popular with visitors. They go above and beyond the call of duty to keep everybody happy.

Kildonan is a small village right next to the sea with views of Pladda Island and Ailsa Craig in the distance. The Kildonan Hotel is right next to the site so is handy for meals if you don't fancy cooking or if you fancy a drink. But here wildlife abounds and you can watch from the van or on a walk along the beach. There are seals just "hauling out", which means chilling out, drying out and warming up before they sink elegantly back into the water. There are also otters playing – frolicking is a word that really suits them when they are in the water as they are all heads and tails. On one occasion we saw a basking shark, the occasional dolphins and big hares in the fields nearby. We saw one hare fighting a crow to protect its young; the crow gave up and flew away. With the sea in front of you and beautiful views behind you this wildlife haven is a gem of a place. We were nearing the end of our trip. We had two nights here then it was back to the mainland and home. That night the stars were twinkling in a clear sky. The air was chilly and as we looked out of the moon window lying in bed, we thought ourselves blessed that we were able to feel so alive and at one with nature and the magic of the heavens. As Abraham Lincoln said, "I can see how it might be possible for a man to look down upon the earth and be an atheist but I cannot conceive how a man can look up into the heavens and say there is no God."

Day 28: Kildonan to Brodick – 12 miles

The next day we said our goodbyes and took the ferry back to Ardrossan. We were headed home but we had decided we would have one night at Herding Hill Farm on Hadrian's Wall, before heading back to our family. We always miss them, but we send our granddaughters each a card every day so they have a little record of where we have been. Then, when we see them, we tell them all the stories about what we have seen and done. I also send my Mam cards because she has Alzheimer's and although she can't always remember, she likes knowing where we are. We are never sad to go home because spending time with family is what we love.

Day 29: Brodick to Ardrossan, then Haltwhistle – 134 miles

Ardrossan is a big town, but to be honest, the way we drive in and out bypasses the city centre because we only ever have time to catch the ferry or tend to want to keep driving if we are going home. So, in all honesty, I have to say they have the ferry port well signed and easy to get to. There is also a big Asda, handy for any last minute items you might need. One day it is my intention to park up and have a look around and do some shopping. So our next and last port of call is a site near Haltwhistle in Northumberland.

Herding Hill Farm is a special site, especially if you like dark skies, lots of stars and all manner of Roman history. It is located on Hadrian's Wall. The site is well organised, the walks nearby are filled with history and the owner is friendly and helpful. We had a good pitch, a relaxing night's sleep and were ready the next day to drive for an hour or so back home.

In all we had travelled about 1300 miles. We thought about where we had been and what we had done and how it had all come about because we had taken the risk and bought Ruby, trusting her maintenance to other people and relying on the good inherent in everybody to sell us what we wanted.

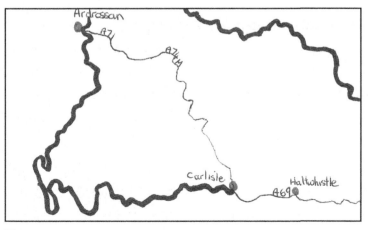

I hope this has encouraged anyone out there who likes

the freedom of the great outdoors and the open road, to make the change and venture out in to the great wide open. Remember William Adams said: "You can have anything you want – if you want it badly enough. You can be anything you want to be, do anything you set out to accomplish if you hold to that desire with singleness of purpose."

List of caravan and campsites where we stayed

Northumberland – Beal
The Barn at Beal Campsite
Beal Farm
Berwick upon Tweed
TD15 2PB
Email: info@the barnatbeal.com
Tel: 01289 540044
Open 360 days of the year

East Lothian – North Berwick
Tantallon Caravan and Camping Park
Dunbar Road
North Berwick
EH39 5NJ
Email: tantallon@meadowhead.co.uk
Tel: 01620 893348

Fife – Lower/Upper Largo
Forth House Caravan Site
Newburn
By Upper Largo
Leven
KY8 6JE
Email: stay@forthhousecaravansite.co.uk
Tel: 07718 788317

Fife – St Andrews
Craigtoun Meadows Holiday Park
Mount Melville
St Andrews
Fife
KY16 8PQ
Email: info@craigtounmeadows.co.uk
Tel: 01334 475959

Aberdeenshire and Kincardinshire – Miltonhaven
Seaside Caravan Park and Campsite
St Cyrus
Montrose
DD10 0DL
Tel: 01674 850413

Scottish Highlands – Inverness
Bunchrew Caravan Park Ltd
Bunchrew
Inverness
IV3 8TD
Email: enquiries@bunchrew.com
Tel: 01463 237802

Scottish Highlands – Fortrose
Fortrose Bay Campsite
Wester Greengates
Fortrose
Ross- Shire
IV10 8RX
Email: fortrosebaycampsite@gmail.com
Tel: 01381 621927

Caithness – Wick
Wick Caravan and Camping Site
Riverside Drive
Wick
KW1 5SP
Caithness
Tel: 01955 605420

Caithness – Dunnet Bay
Dunnet Bay Caravan Club Site
Dunnet
Thurso
Highlands,
KW14 8XD
Tel: 01847 821319

Sutherland – Durness
Sango Sands Oasis
Durness
Sutherland
Highlands
IV27 4PP
Email: keith.durness@btinternet.com
Tel: 01971511262/5112222

Ross and Cromarty – Ullapool
Broomfield Holiday Park
West Lane
Ullapool
IV26 2UT
Tel: 01854 612020

For a quieter, coastal location, I recommend the following site. We have stayed there, but not on this trip.

Ardmair Point Caravan and Camping Park
Ardmair Point
Ullapool
IV26 2TN
Tel: 01854 612054

Wester Ross – Gairloch
Gairloch Caravan Park
1,Mihol Road
Strath
Gairloch
IV21 2BX
Email: info@gairlochcaravanpark.com
Tel: 01445 712373

Inner Hebrides – Isle of Skye.
Portree
Torvaig Caravan and Campsite
Torvaig
Portree
IV51 9HU
Contact: John Maclean
Tel: 01478 611849

Fort William
Glen Nevis Caravan and Camping Park
Glen Nevis
Fort William
PH33 6SX
Email: holidays@glen-nevis.co.uk
Tel: 01397 702191

Inner Hebrides – Isle of Mull
Shieling Holidays
Craignure
Mull
PA65 6AY
Tel: 01680 812496

Fidden Farm Campsite
Knockvologan Road
Near Fionnphort
Isle of Mull
PA66 6BN
Tel: 01681 700427

Kintyre Peninsula – Tayinloan
Point Sands Holiday Park
Tayinloan
Kintyre
Tarbert
PA29 6XG
Email: info@pointsands.com
Tel: 01583 441263

Kintyre Peninsula – Muasdale
Muasdale Holiday Park
Muasdale
Tarbert
Kintyre
Argyll
PA29 6XD
Email: enquiries@muasdaleholidays.com
Tel: 07473 869983 or 01583 421559

Isle of Islay, Inner Hebrides
Port Mòr Centre
Port Charlotte
Isle of Islay
PA48 7UE
Email : warden@islandofislay.co.uk
Tel: 01496 850441

Isle of Arran
Lochranza Campsite and Golf
Lochranza
Isle of Arran
KA27 8HL
Email: info@arran-campsite.com
Tel: 01770 830273

Isle of Arran – Kildonan
Seal Shore Campsite
Kildonan
Isle of Arran
KA27 8SE
Email: enquiries@campingarran.com
Tel : 01770 820320

Haltwhistle
Herding Hill Farm
Shield Hill
Haltwhistle
NE49 9NW
Email: bookings@herdinghillfarm.co.uk
Tel: 01434 320175

Sources

All the information used in this book came from many sources, first of all my own knowledge about the places we visited which I already knew or had read about in books like *The Rough Guide to Scottish Highlands and Islands* (which I think is an excellent read), the people we spoke to when visiting those places and the information we read or heard on tours, in those places while visiting.

I also had to check that what I had written was accurate, using the internet. One website which I found most informative is, 'Undiscovered Scotland'.

The on-line Scottish Tourist board were so helpful when we embarked on our first trip after Jim's chemotherapy. They sent me a list of the A and E hospital departments that were open 24 hours. At that time we had to be within an hour's reach of the nearest one.

I have not copied any other work and apart from the quotes which I have acknowledged, sometimes going to great lengths to find out who said them, this is my own work written from memory and experience, using notes in my diary.

Finally, a heartfelt thank you to my friend Priscilla who helped me with my book.

Printed in Great Britain
by Amazon

23002191R00036